all about
guard
dogs

by
howard h.
hirschhorn

Distributed in the U.S.A. by T.F.H. Publications, Inc., 211 West Sylvania Avenue, P.O. Box 27, Neptune City, N.J. 07753; in England by T.F.H. (Gt. Britain) Ltd., 13 Nutley Lane, Reigate, Surrey; in Canada to the book store and library trade by Clarke, Irwin & Company, Clarwin House, 791 St. Clair Avenue West, Toronto 10, Ontario; in Canada to the pet trade by Rolf C. Hagen Ltd., 3225 Sartelon Street, Montreal 382, Quebec; in Southeast Asia by Y.W. Ong, 9 Lorong 36 Geylang, Singapore 14; in Australia and the south Pacific by Pet Imports Pty. Ltd., P.O. Box 149, Brookvale 2100, N.S.W., Australia. Published by T.F.H. Publications Inc. Ltd., The British Crown Colony of Hong Kong.

CONTENTS

INTRODUCTION

It was no mortal poet's mere fancy to set a three-headed dog—Cerberus—on guard duty at the gates of Hades. It was not a thirty-foot crocodile or Siberian tiger or King Kong gorilla, or even a man, which thousands of years of legend considered capable of enforcing the rules of entry to the universe's most damned spot. A dog, no less, it was. And with three heads.

The dog was cradled (along with the louse and a few other less lovable creatures) along with man from the beginning. The dog can become a savage beast upon command. . . but can still remain subject to man's voice and even mind. The guard dog, the sentry dog, the war dog, the police dog, the attack dog. . . all of these share the function of extending man's vigilance and exercise of legitimate force.

The Viking warriors, for example, loved their dogs. To these Norse fighters, dogs were warriors, trackers, herders, guards and protectors.

VIKING DOGS BEFORE 1000 A.D.

Many dogs were kept for guard service in the old Nordic countries during and before the time of the Vikings. Intensive cattle raising by off-season sailors on Iceland, for example, required dogs. A cattle-owning chieftain had much to guard during the frequent famines.

Strong, courageous, perceptive dogs were highly prized for pathfinding. One Norse traveler, an overnight guest at an Icelandic farmhouse, was accompanied on his way in the morning by the farmer's tracking dog; the dog brought the guest safely through a forest, then trotted back to his master's farmhouse.

A noted tale of a thousand years ago tells of Olaf giving Gunnar a large dog which possessed almost human powers of reasoning. His master's friends were his friends and his master's enemies were his enemies. "You are now Gunnar's dog," Olaf said when he presented the dog to Gunnar. The dog then went straight to his new master and lay down at his feet. Thereafter the dog was as loyal to its new master as he had been to Olaf. Gunnar's enemies were kept at bay for many years, daring to attack and kill Gunnar only after they had managed to kill his dog first. Gunnar's attachment to his dog was supposed to have been so strong that Gunnar sprang up from his sleep to warn his dog just as the animal let out his death cry. Gunnar was soon assassinated thereafter.

Norway once had four treasures , it has been said, and these were a certain king, his wife Thyra, his warship Orm and his wardog Wigi. Dog and king were as close as brothers. When news came of the king's death at the battle of Svoldur, one of the king's vassals said to Wigi, "Wigi, we have no more master," whereupon the dog made its way up to a hilltop, stretched out and remained there until it died of starvation days later.

RESPONSIBILITY ASSOCIATED WITH OWNING A PROTECTION DOG

A highly trained protection dog is usually a one-man (or one-woman) dog. Notice we say *man* or *woman, not child*. A capable child who knows how to treat a dog, however, can learn to train a dog for obedience, that is, to sit, stay, heel, lie down, come. A protection dog must be skillfully managed (along with supplying the love it needs). Unmanaged, it can get out of hand and turn into a menace, not only to its immediate family but the public. Then, dear dog lover, you are a candidate for legal action and perhaps a loss of your patiently and lovingly and expensively trained animal.

Some protective action by your dog is instinctive, and needs only encouragement, proper training, and management. The bitch, an owner soon observes, can be beautifully gentle when all is going well, but viciously aggressive when her own litter or her own home is threatened. A large

A fence is as good as what guards it. Snarling, however, is not the proper image of a good watchdog. A good watchdog should not be vicious. . . but it is trained to seem that way sometimes. Photo courtesy of Security Dogs, Hialeah, Florida.

breed of dog tends to interpose itself between master and stranger. Quite reassuring for the master. Quite frightening for the stranger. A protection dog can develop quite spontaneously into an attack dog.

WHAT IS THE BEST BREED FOR PROTECTION?

Medium to large working and sporting breeds are generally suitable for guard, police or war dog training. Degree of intelligence and pugnaciousness of individual dogs, of course, will determine whether a particular one of these breeds will meet an individual owner's needs concerning deterrent looks, viciousness (a well-trained dog should not really be vicious) and real attack power. There is a thin

The Doberman Pinscher (also spelled Dobermann) originated from a more impetuous and fiery breed than did the German Shepherd, and this is more of a one-man dog than the German Shepherd. Some people consider the Dobie to be more threatening than the Shepherd as a guard dog. Photo courtesy of Security Dogs, Hialeah, Florida.

line between protecting and attacking—defense necessarily becomes attack when the potential aggressor refuses to be scared off by gnashing teeth and barking of a guard dog and advances to seize the dog's owner. So keep in mind when you choose your breed exactly what kind of protection service you will need.

Sporting dogs and gundogs are usually good natured and also make good family and house dogs. A Golden Re-

The Labrador Retriever, being a large size breed (60 lbs. or more), will make a good guard dog. In addition to the ability to retrieve, many other desirable characteristics are found in this breed as well. Photo courtesy of Winchester-Western Division, Olin Mathieson Chemical Corporation.

triever, Trep*, was the Dade County (Miami, Florida) Sheriff's Department narcotics dog which sniffed out 2,439 pounds of hashish valued at two million dollars (retail value, and $250,000 at wholesale value). The contraband drug was seized on March 4, 1974 aboard a forty-eight foot racing schooner at Ft. Lauderdale, Florida. An alert, active dog with an even temper, the Golden Retriever is a loyal and easily trained dog.

Powerfully set and intelligent Chesapeake Bay Retrie-

* The dog's trainer was Officer Tom Kazo, Dade County Sheriff's Department.

A pair of Rhodesian Ridgebacks showing the characteristic ridge on the back. When trained for hunting they are fearless, aggressive dogs but for the home they are loyal, obedient dogs.

The Bull Terrier was bred for fighting in Medieval times. It is thought of as the strongest breed of dog. Photo by S.A. Thompson.

The Rottweiler may not appear menacing but the police work record of this breed is firmly established along with other breeds used for police work.

A Rottweiler being trained for holding.

In their original habitat (Siberia and Arctic Russia) Samoyeds were outstanding protectors of their aboriginal masters.

It may not be wise to allow any puppy such as this tiny Samoyed to play with shoes. This cute activity may turn out to be more of a nuisance later.

Belgian Sheepdogs are not too well known in the United States where German Shepherds predominate in popularity as guard dogs.

The unusual large size of the Saint Bernard is depicted very well in this photo. A would-be intruder can easily be discouraged by this feature alone.

vers are more resilient to the kiddies who may roll and tumble a bit too much for some other breeds. This natural retriever loves hunting in and about water, despite freezing temperatures and ice. Their sense of smell is superb. Their memory allows them to keep several birds in mind as they go afield to fetch the bird their master shoots. They rarely fail to retrieve. A Chesapeake Bay Retriever is easily trained by its owner, and works best for that person alone.

The kind faced Labrador Retriever possesses excellent scenting ability, great stamina and love of water.

Shown is a fine example of the Bloodhound breed, Champion Doctor Watson of Baker Street.

These dogs are seeing eye dogs, "paradogs" (parachute duty with the Armed Forces), trackers of loiterers in London's Hyde Park and guards at Buckingham Palace!

The "gray ghosts" or Weimaraners are by temperament and flexibility quite suitable as watchdogs as well as homebodies (not doing their best as kennel dogs, however), and also as hunting dogs on either fur or feather.

The Bloodhound in an affectionate, tailwagging specialist whose proverbial olfactory sense will lead police to their man . . . and who will then bay away in a profuse and gentle joy of having found its quarry, frightening the fugitive only by its persistent baying, but not by any snarling attitude, except as noted below in a report written in 1859 by Goodrich (in his *Illustrated Natural History of the Animal Kingdom being a Systematic and Popular Description of the Habits, Structure, and Classification of Animals from the Highest to the Lowest Forms, with their Relation to Agriculture, Commerce, Manufactures and the Arts,* Volume I, New York: Derby & Jackson):

"The perseverance and sagacity (of the English Bloodhound) in following a man on whose track they had often been set, often for miles, even through towns and villages and crowded thoroughfares, was indeed wonderful. In general, when they found the culprits, they would patiently keep guard over them, and not permit them to move away until their masters came up. Sometimes, however, dogs of ferocious disposition would fall upon them and tear them in pieces. The manner in which the Bloodhound pursued the robber is thus described by the poet Somerville:

> "Soon the sagacious brute, his curling tail
> Flourish'd in air, low bending, plies around
> His busy nose, the steaming vapor snuffs
> Inquisitive, nor leaves one turf untried,
> Till, conscious of the recent stains, his heart
> Beats quick. His snuffing nose, his active tail,
> Attest his joy. Then, with deep opening mouth,
> That makes the welkin tremble, he proclaims
> Th' audacious felon. Foot by foot he marks
> His winding way. Over the watery ford,
> Dry sandy heaths, and stony barren hills,
> Unerring he pursues, till at the cot
> Arrived, and, seizing by his guilty throat
> The caitiff vile, redeems the captive prey."

The Bullmastiff was initially bred for the purpose of guarding property against poachers in the middle part of the 18th century in England.

The Great Pyrenees breed is another sheepdog-type known for its gentleness, coupled with the main trait of protectiveness, which is usually present in sheepherding dogs.

The Basenji may not be desirable as a watchdog as it is a non-barking dog. In addition, it is also a small dog.

A family of Bouvier des Flandres. Bouviers are cattle herders and must prove their ability to work in order to qualify as representatives of the breed in dog shows in Belgium today.

"Before the union between England and Scotland, the "border" between the two countries was the theater of constant forays for the purpose of stealing sheep, cattle, and other property. The English and Scotch were, in fact, as great robbers as the Bedouins of the present day. In this state of things the Bloodhounds became indispensable as guards. The pursuit of border forayers was called the 'hot-trod'. The harried party and his friends followed the marauders with Bloodhounds and bugle-horn, and if his dog could trace the scent into the opposite kingdom, he was entitled to pursue them thither."

Three rugged, veldt-living Rhodesian Ridgebacks will fearlessly charge a pride of five lions. These muscular, aggressive dogs nevertheless make fine protectors of home and child.

The Irish Wolfhound is friendly to man, child and beast. Yet he challenges trespassers, growls deeply and threateningly, then, if this is not heeded, latches onto the aggressor (rather than biting or tearing at him).

The Saluki—thought to be the oldest breed of domesticated dog—has been used successfully as a watchdog as well as its prime jobs of coursing at up to fifty miles per hour after gazelle, hares and other quarry. Salukis are believed to be the dogs appearing on Egyptian walls (2100 B.C.), and Sumerian buildings (7000 to 6000 B.C.).

Alaskan Malamutes are affectionate family dogs who are playful but tend to be reserved. They do bark convincingly, though.

Groenendahls, Tervurens and Malinois—all Belgian sheepdogs—train easily and possess fine temperament for being guard dogs, seeing-eye dogs and pets in general. Although not anxious, these dogs tend to be quite attentive to the presence of strangers.

Another Belgian Champ, the Bouvier, must hold a police, military or guard dog working title before it can achieve bench show championship. Cattle driving, medical corps litter pulling and wartime messenger service are other jobs the Bouvier (des Flandres) has to its credit.

Boxers, originally bull-baiting dogs, make good watchdogs as well as reliable pets.

The goat-like, hairy Briard has herded sheep and other animals, pulled wagons and served as police and war dog.

The "gamekeeper's nightdog" or Bullmastiff was developed as a quiet, guard-attack dog to throw and hold (not bite or tear) dangerous poachers (the ones who began shooting at gamekeepers rather than be caught and given stiff punishment). This affectionate dog performed sentry duty without vicious attitudes or biting.

Doberman Pinschers are excellent guard, police and war dogs as well as fine companions, tending to be one-man dogs, although they are fine family watchdogs, too.

The German Shepherd needs no introduction as a watchdog, companion, house dog, police and war dog, seeing-eye dog, and herding dog. It is *the* stereotype of *the* guard dog.

The Giant Schnauzer makes a fine protection and police dog.

The Great Dane has hunted boar and guarded property (not necessarily through aggressiveness, but mere size and build).

The Great Pyrenees is an apt protector of property and herds. It has also been used as a draft dog for sleds and carts.

The shaggy, outdoor Komondor is a guard dog for home and property. Its wooly coat tends to form cords, thus adding a distinctive character to this breed.

The Mastiff has been long used as a watchdog, war dog, herder, bear-baiting dog, companion and hunter.

The gentle, lumbering Newfoundland has been watchdog, guard, companion, draft and pack dog, and, particularly, rescuer of shipwrecked seamen. This dog is a fine swimmer and diver, even capable of swimming underwater, a valuable asset in stormy seas or water which is covered with burning oil.

The friendly, shaggy Old English Sheepdog has herded cattle and sheep quite successfully.

The Puli, another shaggy, sheepherding and companion dog, is wary of the approach of strangers, thus making a name for itself as a family watchdog.

Rottweilers policed the herds of cattle which went along with the Roman legions. This solidly built and obedient dog has performed admirably as police and family watchdog.

The size of the huge, affectionate St. Bernard, not its aggressiveness, acts as a deterrent to a potential attacker.

A trio of Salukis. One of the oldest dog breeds, the Saluki's ancestry dates back to the time of the Pharaohs. Being a galloping type, these dogs require plenty of exercise.

A muzzle has been placed on this female Saluki for precautionary reasons during breeding. A female in heat is apt to bite the male.

This photo of an Irish Wolfhound with a trio of kittens portrays the proportions of this breed. Great size is desired by breeders. Although utilized for hunting the Wolfhound is not aggressive.

The snow-white Samoyed reindeer dogs or "smiling" dogs are sled, herding and companion dogs, as well as good guards.

Friendly, powerful Bull Terriers or "White Cavaliers" were originally bred as fighters. General Patton had one. Richard Harding Davis wrote of the breed in his *The Bar Sinister*. Jock, a police Bull Terrier of Nairobi, seized onto a sword-wielding criminal (from whom he received seven wounds, requiring three dozen sutures) until the man was subdued and arrested.

Alert and docile (to people, but not to other animals!) Staffordshire Terriers, like Bull Terriers, were bred as fighters, and are therefore apparently less sensitive to the pain of injury.

The Collie is a reliable housedog and child's guardian.

Dalmatians make excellent family, sentry, guard and watchdogs. Circus shows, too, have been graced by the spotted coach dogs.

Although the Keeshond or Dutch barge dog is a smaller breed, it rendered good watchdog duty on river and canal vessels.

Australian Shepherds, although a smaller breed, are natural guard dogs. They snap quickly when required, but are otherwise gentle and easily trained.

YOUR NEW PUPPY

When you first bring your pup home, it may lose its playfulness for awhile amid strange smells and surroundings. Expect it to piddle from excitement, fear or right after meals. You can tell when it is about to piddle because it runs in circles several times, sniffs about and finally squats to piddle. The presence of an older dog in your home may cause a problem or may not. Older dogs sometimes resent younger ones for awhile, but they also make training the new puppy much easier because the young pup tends to follow the example given by the older dog.

Lift your puppy properly. Do not lift him by his front legs as these are still very tender and may be disjointed by having to support his weight. Lift him with a hand under his rump and a hand under his chest and try to hold him close to you when you pick him up.

Start training immediately. Take advantage of your puppy's instinctive desire to please you. A good strong *no! no!* should punctuate his first piddling, for example. Give him a friendly pat as you call him by name and he comes to you (he'll come to you not because of the name but because he is merely doing what all puppies do, that is, coming to a friendly person.)

Provide a safe and comfortable sleeping nook for your new puppy. The sleeping spot should not be high off the ground and should be warm enough to keep the dog from shivering if it is the cold season. Do not pamper it if it cries at night. Use a ticking clock or, as some owners do, soft music to keep it company. Place several pages of newspaper nearby to begin the dog's newspaper training.

Avoid stairways: puppy bones are soft, sutures in the skull are open, and joints and muscles are still undeveloped. Avoid drafts: puppies catch colds easily. Avoid other dogs, too, until you see your veterinarian; your pup's first visit should be within a week of your obtaining him. Your

An old tennis ball can provide pleasure and training for a young dog when associated with the right command. Photo courtesy of Three Lions.

A successfully trained dog will heed its master's commands under any circumstances. Photo courtesy of Three Lions.

Training a Doberman puppy requires knowledge and prudence. Improper training can transform this puppy into a potentially dangerous animal.

vet will advise you as to the pup's health and the required immunizations.

Puppy playtime is beautiful, but exhausting to the puppy. Tell children that the puppy will play until it cannot stand up, and that they should let it rest every fifteen or twenty minutes. Too much activity after meals may cause a puppy to vomit. Rough play could teach the pup to nip. Tug-of-war could also be played to extremes, that is, take care that the puppy does not learn to pull tablecloths, curtains, or electric cords because it has been trained too well in a game of tug-of-war.

Retrieving a ball makes use of the puppy's natural tendency. Encourage it. And make its future fetching lessons easier for both you and the dog. You should continue practicing with the puppy's name so that it learns to come when its name is mentioned. The puppy will appreciate a squeaking toy (and there are many made just for dogs), and some household items, providing that you check their safety beforehand. Shoes, for example, can be dangerous because of the toxic substances used to dye them as well as the metal and other hard materials built into them. Also, once the dog gets used to chewing on shoes, no shoe will be safe in the house. Teething pups (four to five months) appreciate nylon bones. These can be obtained at any pet shop. There are also substances available which discourage the dog from chewing on objects not meant to be chewed upon in the house. Nylabone is a safe substitute for real bones and is highly recommended as being healthy for dogs' gums, etc.

Other equipment or supplies needed would include non-tipping pans for food and water. Leashes, too, should be bought at this time. There are three lengths available: a short traffic leash (about one and one-half feet long), a walking and training leash (four to six feet), a longer leash for training purposes or for allowing the dog more freedom on the lawn (twelve to fifteen feet along). An overhead pulley and trolley arrangement allows a dog to run over the lawn without getting tangled up in his leash.

It may take several minutes to accustom your wildly twisting pup to tolerate a collar. Check collars frequently on fast growing breeds. You should be able to slip about two fingers under properly adjusted collars. Flea collars will protect your dog against fleas.

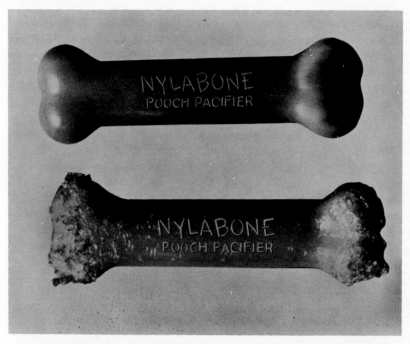

Nylabone, a synthetic substitute for real chew bones, is not only tasty (meat flavor incorporated into it) but also not liable to break up into dangerous chips or splinters.

Let the pup drag his new leash around his home awhile before walking, and it soon becomes associated with the pleasurable activity of going outside. Your pup will soon learn to get it himself whenever you make a move toward the door.

As soon as your pup is protected by inoculations, socialization may begin. Socialization is the dog's learning to fit into the context of life around it and the people in its family. Take it to as many places as you can (without breaking any laws.)

Do not create inhibitions in your pup by leaving it alone all the time. If a pup under six months of age is always left in the garage or apartment, it may become timid and hide when guests arrive. Or, on the other hand, it could even become overly protective and aggressive.

A Weimaraner being trained not to pursue moving vehicles. The "gun" is an ordinary water pistol. Photo Courtesy of Three Lions.

Opposite, upper photo:
A pair of Komondors. The fur of this dog breed tends to mat and form cords.

Opposite, lower photo:
The Puli is another shaggy dog. It is also considered to be a reliable watchdog.

Do not strike your animal in anger. Yet, do not waste more than a minute or so before punishing it, or at least reprimanding it, for a misdeed. A dog, like a child, simply does not remember why it is being punished if one waits too long. Also, if your dog does not come immediately when you call it, but comes later, avoid punishing it; it will associate punishment with coming when called. Rather, go after it when it does not come, then you can tell the dog it is a *bad dog*, or use another reasonable and workable disciplinary measure.

Although a tap on the muzzle or an offending paw is appropriate discipline, verbal reprimand, coupled at times with a newspaper slap against your own leg to gain attention, is much better in the long run than is striking the dog.

NO, NO! or BAD DOG! is an essential phrase in training a dog. Here, a dog responds merely to the trainer's hand signal for BAD DOG.

Upon occasion, however, when dog and master know each other's limits and mentalities, an appropriate (and controlled!) slap is not out of the question.

Your puppy will go through a period of rapid growth over its first eight months. From the first to the third month it is still shaky on its legs, fun-loving and mischievous. From the fourth to the fifth month it begins to lose its milk teeth. It may become touchy because of the sore gums associated with the change in dentition. At six months your puppy is a half-grown dog, quite perceptive and possessing a voracious appetite. Some states require a license at this age. From the eighth to the eleventh month your dog is three-quarters grown and almost rid of its ungainliness, but beginning to show some willfulness. Female dogs may begin to show their first bleeding at this time. The bleeding lasts for up to about three weeks. The puppy coat is shed and there may be a slight color change appearing in the new coat. From the eleventh to the thirteenth month your puppy's height is maximal, but its chest and muscles still have to be developed. The dog then passes through an episode of stubbornness. Good training *before* this period prepares both you and the dog to get through this headstrong period without too much unpleasantness. Your dog, like you, will have good and bad days, too.

As a final thought on puppy care you should be aware that tattooing of a number and/or name in the ear or on the inner part of the dog's thigh is a positive legal identification. A research institution confronted with an offer of sale rejects any dog with a tattoo.

A slight reprimand is enough to discourage a very intelligent breed like the Poodle from leaping on anybody.

Three sizes of Poodle: Standard, Miniature, and Toy.

One of the taller breeds, a Great Dane, can be more than 32 inches high at the shoulders. Without doubt any dog of this size can impress most prowlers about the home.

A young Dalmatian being trained to jump. Note that an ordinary cot can be used as a barrier to overcome.

In spite of the St. Bernard's huge size, dogs of this breed are very friendly. "Tierfunde" photo.

TRAINING PHASES

Obedience training precedes other training. The dog must listen and respond to its master. Otherwise it becomes useless as a work dog, and may become burdensome and even a public danger.

Protection training is the defensive phase of training for the dog. Attack training, also, can be considered protective training. It is obvious that a good offense is sometimes the best defense, that is, what do you do when an aggressor refuses to stop when warned by your dog's presence, full show of teeth and bark? What you do *not* want to do, of course, in a civilian and peacetime situation, is to destroy the enemy! Even police dogs are not trained to do that, but rather to deter, capture (and release!), subdue, and guard (both the suspect and the policeman!). Going after a would be assailant's weapon or a raised arm could certainly be considered a defensive maneuver.

There are also training phases for teaching the dog to take advantage of its natural tracking powers. Sight tracing usually seems (to human senses) more exciting than tracking. A track of scent, however, is just as vivid to the dog's sense of smell as a fleeing assailant is to our sense of vision. Searching, too, involves finding something or someone, but requires the dog to follow airborne scent rather than follow a line of scent along a ground track.

Sections on obedience, protection, attack, tracking and searching training follow.

OBEDIENCE TRAINING

A WORD OF CAUTION

The first requirement for training a dog is to be smarter than the dog. This is no joke. You may be more intelligent or experienced than the dog, but the dog may still outwit you. If you are prone to fits of anger when someone (particularly a dog) outsmarts you, then decide to improve yourself. Get smarter, or become more patient. If that is beyond you, give up before you ruin a good dog, and go to a professional handler for help. Know your dog's personality—shy or nervous, bullish, clown, lazy, naive—and adjust yourself accordingly.

At three to four months of age, your pup is still small enough to be handled easily, and malleable enough to learn well. Obedience training is best started by the fifth to sixth month of age.

Training consists of periods of repetition and reward for at least ten minutes daily, perhaps even several ten-minute periods, depending upon your patience and that of your dog.

The dog's training period should be given before it eats. Obedience lessons are designed to teach the dog to heel, sit, stay, lie down, and come. (*No* should have been taught long before, at the first piddle on your living room rug!)

COLLAR AND CHOKER

The choker, when put on properly, tightens when the dog strains away from you and loosens when the dog ceases to pull away.

The Boxer is a breed worth considering as a
watchdog. Boxers appear ferocious and can scare
intruders easily.

Opposite:
In addition to being a good sporting dog, the
German Shorthaired Pointer is also a good house
and watchdog.

GIVING COMMANDS

Speak in an even voice, repeating several times if necessary. Precede the command with the dog's name, except for the command to *STAY*. This helps to distinguish it from *SIT*, and also gives you a quickly given command for emergency use.

Reward a successful response with praise or a pat, and occasional tidbits. Do not rub in the failures, but try to overlook them.

Thoroughly grasp each "trick" or exercise before introducing the dog to the next one.

Dogs, like their owners, have differences in alertness, response and sensitivity. Give a dog several moments to respond.

The owner's own reactions and ways of doing and saying things must be consistently the same. Inconsistencies confuse the dog in training.

Command clearly, and preferably in single syllables. Not voice volume but the quality of the tone commands best. A quietly given command causes the dog to pay more attention and to focus its concentration on the command. Make the first command stick. Repetitions are not good, obviously, for immediate results are desired from the first command.

Do not permit your dog to ignore or fail to carry out a command.

Introduce and try out all new commands while your dog is on the leash, under your control; thus immediate corrections can be made in faulty responses.

Corporal punishment, that is, striking the dog hard, is only for rare, if any, emergencies. Reliance should be placed, instead, on patience, an appropriate tug on the choke chain and leash, and spoken admonition and praise.

Stop a training session when the dog's interest lags.

It is important to end each training session on a happy note. You may even have to go back to an easier command in order to end cleanly with a response that the dog knows well and enjoys doing.

To begin, the dog goes on your left side. Hold the leash in your right hand, but let it pass across your front, through your left hand, which is held down near the dog.

Learning to HEEL.

An American breed, the Chesapeake Bay Retriever, is easy to train. Many outstanding champions are known which did not require specialized training by professionals.

Opposite:
Except for the reduced size, the attributes of a Shetland Sheepdog parallel those of the Collie.
Photo by Dr. Herbert R. Axelrod.

When teaching your dog to HEEL, STOP or STAY, encourage it by caressing or scratching under the muzzle or behind the ears, whenever it stops and waits for you. It should learn to expect pleasantness by following your orders promptly.

Learning to SIT. Gentle pressure on the dog's back helps it to understand what is wanted.

HEEL

Say the dog's name, then command *HEEL* to the dog, standing at your left side. Pull back and snap on the leash if he darts ahead or to the side. Avoid playing tug-of-war with your dog. Speak in an even tone, repeating as often as necessary.

Use your left hand to scratch or pat your dog a bit whenever it is in proper position. Once in the proper posi-

The heavy set Giant Schnauzer has been used for
police work. It is a popular dog in the southern
parts of Germany.

Opposite:
Close-up of a harlequin patterned Great Dane.
Photo by Dr. Herbert R. Axelrod.

Guard duty is a task which can be confidently assigned to a Staffordshire Terrier. It is a breed of strong and muscular dogs originally developed for pit fighting in England.

tion, the dog should expect no pulling or discomfort, but only praise and comfort. It thus knows proper performance is associated with pleasure.

A "well-heeled" dog trots happily along at your left side, his right shoulder near your left knee. Let the dog lead you for awhile, if necessary, until it becomes accustomed to the leash. Once mastered, heeling can be done at different speeds and with frequent change of direction.

Progress when ready to free heeling, that is, heeling without the leash.

SIT

Once your dog knows how to heel, and is walking along at your side properly, stop. Take up slack in the leash with your right hand, press down with your left hand on the dogs hindquarters, saying the dog's name and *SIT*. Wait a moment. Then, if the dog has not responded, pull down on the leash and force the dog's hindquarters down to show it just what you want it to do. Praise the dog for successfully sitting down. When forcing the dog to sit down, be certain you are pressing down on its rump (or croup). Pressure elsewhere, particularly over the kidneys, causes pain. Too much of the painful pushing down could make the dog handshy.

A properly installed choker on a Staffordshire Terrier.

Periodic inoculations are indispensable for any dog.

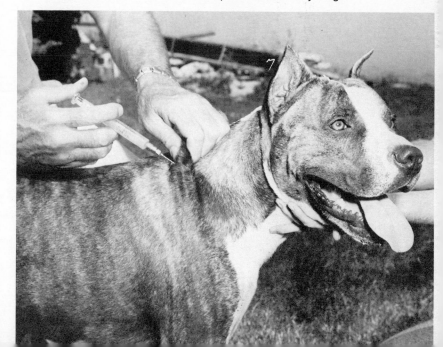

The Tervuren is considered as a mere color variant of the Belgian Sheepdog although it is expected to possess all the fine qualities of the famous European sheepherder. Photo by Edeltraud Laurin.

Whether in its corded or combed-out coat, the Puli is an intelligent, energetic dog that is adaptable to training of many different kinds. Photo by Evelyn Shafer.

Learning to SIT in the (already learned) heeling position. Note that the trainer's left hand exerts some control near the collar.

Have your dog heel and sit in repeated practice sessions spaced apart so as to avoid boredom and exhaustion for both of you. When these two commands are well understood and executed, go on to the command *STAY*.

STAY

SIT is prolonged into *STAY,* that is, the dog remains sitting despite your moving away from it. Tell it to *SIT*. Hold the leash in your right hand, put your left palm in front of its nose. Command *STAY!* (Remember, no name usually precedes this command.) Make one step forward with your right foot, turn about and face the dog. Repulse any forward movement of the dog by repeating the command, pushing it into the sitting position. Hold your right hand in front of its nose again as a reminder. Then, after a moment, take your place at its side again.

In successive training periods, gradually move further away (letting the leash run loosely over your hands) until

Learning to STAY at a distance. The trainer must concentrate fully on the dog, discouraging any tendency to follow. No tension is applied to the leash.

Corgies have been reported to give up their own
lives for the protection of their masters. Photo by
Laurence Larkin.

Opposite:
The fearsome appearance of a Bulldog may be the
feature desired by some individuals in their
choice of guard dogs.

The leash is finally dropped to the ground as soon as the dog knows what is wanted.

you are as far back as the leash permits (keep holding it during these repetitions). After awhile, as you come back to the dog, pass on its left side and around behind it, holding the leash on the dog's right side to keep it clear of wrapping around its body. Finally, do the same maneuver, but at the end of your longest leash (as long as 20 to 30 feet), and waiting a moment before coming back to the dog.

Concentrate fully on the dog as you move away during these exercises; correct each mistake instantly as it is made. For this exercise, do not call or let the dog come to you; you return to it, so it learns to wait for you.

After the dog has learned to stay as long as you are in sight, it must then learn to stay without seeing you. It should always be rewarded by seeing that, in fact, you do come back, bringing much praise for it as you come.

STAND

STAND is similar to *STAY*, and is sometimes taught before it. A dog which is heeling is gradually brought to a halt. Command *STAND*, place your right hand in front of the dog's nose and caress the dog with your left hand from the withers (or base of the neck) down to the rump. If the dog tries to sit, exert a slight lifting pressure under the dog's body. (See further below under STOPPING and STANDING.)

A dog soon learns to stand quietly for its daily brushing, which is a necessity for some of the longer-haired breeds.

A pair of young Dobermans with their ears still taped. The ears are trimmed to keep them upright all the time.

The ancestors of the Keeshond breed were kept in Holland primarily as house pets and watchdogs.

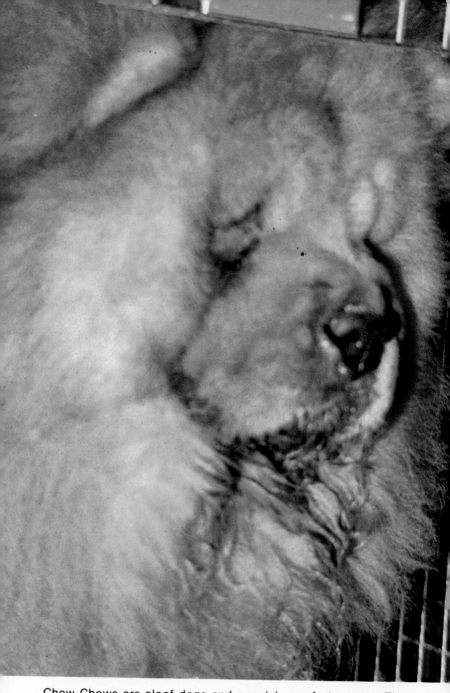

Chow Chows are aloof dogs and suspicious of strangers. They seem to bestow their loyalty on one person alone. Photo by Dr. Herbert R. Axelrod.

LIE DOWN

Kneel down next to your sitting dog. Hold the leash, close to the collar, in your right hand. Say the dog's name and *LIE DOWN*!, bringing the dog's neck down by pulling down your right hand (holding the leash near the collar), and pressing down with your left hand on your dog's shoulders. Keep up the pull if your dog resists, and wait until *you* win. Quickly reward him with *GOOD BOY* (or *GIRL*)! Practice this position from different starting positions, for example, from heeling and from sitting.

Learning to LIE DOWN.
Below: Applying a gentle pull downwards.
Opposite, above: Coaxing all the way down to show the dog exactly what is wanted.
Opposite, below: Completed position of LIE DOWN.

A Briard photographed in the environs of a dog show. Briards are still utilized as hunting and guard dogs in the rural parts of Europe.

Sheep herding dogs, such as Collies, Komondors, Pulis, etc., are all dependable dogs. A pair, like these sheepherders relaxing in a field of wild flowers, can easily take care of a flock of sheep. Colour Library International photo.

If a dog has a propensity to leap in or out of open car windows (a very dangerous act, especially leaping out), attempt to train the dog to do it only upon command. Here, the dog has learned to wait for a command before jumping into the car.

COME

Command your dog to *SIT*, and then to *STAY* while on the longest leash that you have. Then call in your best, most friendly tone, *COME!* You may have to pull a bit to show what is wanted. Keep up encouraging praise as your dog comes closer and take up the slack in the line. Reserve final praise for when the dog is sitting in front of you, precisely just where you want it.

Insist upon instantaneous obedience at all times, or at least keep it in mind as a goal as you patiently urge your dog to instantaneously obey.

A dog learning to seize and hold. The dog has just succeeded in grasping the trainer's jacket. Photo courtesy of Security Dogs, Hialeah, Florida.

This dog quickly gets the proper bite on the trainer's arm which is padded under the jacket. Photo courtesy of Security Dogs, Hialeah, Florida.

A police dog is sometimes left sitting at the open window of a patrol car; the dog waits until its master orders it to COME, even if he is at some distance from his patrol car. Upon hearing the command to COME, or its name, the dog leaps through the open window and immediately joins its master, ready for instant action.

As a variation to the above "most friendly tone" for calling your dog, note that some trainers call *COME* with an *urgent* tone of voice.

Another variation, too, that some trainers employ, is to train the dog to come satisfactorily, and then carry the response a step further by having the dog sit when it arrives without insisting too much that the dog sit during the first lessons.

It is important to remember that if you have difficulty in having your dog come, do not reprimand it when it finally does come to you. Always praise it for coming, otherwise it will associate punishment with the act of coming.

CONTINUING BASIC OBEDIENCE

STOPPING AND STANDING

Your dog should stop and remain standing while you stop to mail a letter, speak with a friend or look at a tree or into a store window. Stop suddenly, keeping a tense leash. When the dog also stops pulling and waits with you, pet it and praise it. It should wait, standing, until you start walking again. At that moment, slacken the leash to indicate it is time to go again. Say *"LET'S GO"* or some similar phrase. Soon your dog will be glancing back at you frequently to see if you are satisfied with its performance. Praise and pet it each time.

OFF-LEASH PHASE

After your dog performs satisfactorily all of the lessons in obedience training covered so far, try the commands without using the leash. Use an enclosed yard or other large, fenced-in area until you and your dog are confident enough of one another.

ANTI-CHASE LESSONS

Dogs naturally love to run. . . after other dogs, cats, their own tails, or merely for the joy of streaking across open spaces.

When your dog darts away after something, it should return—after the first few moments of elated freedom—upon the command *COME*. Pet your dog and give the impression that you are forgiving this transgression. Prepare

Dogs trying again to close on the "assailant." Photo courtesy of Security Dogs, Hialeah, Florida.

The dog leaps to seize hold of the trainer's arm. Photo courtesy of Security Dogs, Hialeah, Florida.

A Doberman, although usually considered a one-man dog, can be a loving family dog, too. Photo courtesy of Security Dogs, Hialeah, Florida.

Any activity accomplished correctly by a dog being trained, such as this Dachshund puppy, should be promptly rewarded by tender handling or words spoken clearly and softly.

A dog's natural actions can be utilized when training it. This dog loves to stand on top of "her" car. With a little coaxing, she learned a new trick—to crouch low on the roof of the car before springing down (opposite). This new trick, however, was learned unintentionally: when the dog's mistress commanded DOWN! to make the dog jump off of the car's roof, the dog understood LIE DOWN!, a command she already knew, so she obediently lay down just where she was. Then the command OFF was practiced until she learned it meant "jump down from up there."

for the next time like this: attach a long line (about ten feet long) to the collar in addition to the regular leash. When your dog next breaks into an unexpected dash, drop the regular leash, but do not drop the long line. The dog will jerk to a sudden stop at the end of the line. Make a great fuss as you approach your dog, commisserating with the frightening jolt just received, just as if you do not know more about what happened than the dog knows. After half a dozen of these jolts, most dogs realize that such shocks do not occur when they stay near their masters. This is one of the activities which demonstrates that *you* are smarter than the dog!

Chasing a car (when not in hot pursuit of an assailant) is a dangerous occupation. Break your dog's habit of this chasing by enlisting the aid of a friend who will drive by to entice your dog into chasing. . . and, when your dog streaks out after the car, will "shoot" the dog in the face with a water pistol.

A good, strong leash and collar must back up the training of a dog. Immediate response must be impressed upon the dog, and a leash is the non-verbal tie between man and dog before the dog learns to obey (and before the human being training it learns to command it). The photo shows a collar and leash suitable for training a dog of this size. Photo courtesy of Security Dogs, Hialeah, Florida.

No one in his right mind will try to scale *this* low fence. Photo courtesy of Security Dogs, Hialeah, Florida.

Commercial kennels with an open-air run. Photo courtesy of Security Dogs, Hialeah, Florida.

The required attitude for showing is not an inbred trait. It is the result of patient training by owners of potential dog champions. Photo by Al Berry from Thee Lions, Inc.

ANTI-JUMP LESSONS

A dog which leaps up on you (or up on frightened and/or resentful guests) is a liability, despite its loving attention.

Bring up your knee suddenly when the dog jumps, letting it strike your knee with its chest. This shock causes the dog to rebound and fall back, astounded as to what happened. It soon learns that uninvited leaps upon people cause an unpleasant bumping. The dog does not associate its ricocheting off of you with your knee; it cannot see your knee go up.

The natural tendency of this dog is to go for feet whenever one of the children in her family rides piggyback. Some herding dogs have been bred to nip at the heels of livestock in order to keep the herd or flock under control. One theory is that this breeding causes Shelties —Shetland Sheepdogs– for example, to go after the feet of bicyclists as a sort of frustrated expression of their breeding. Perhaps such dogs might be more easily trained to go after feet, then, instead of arms, when chasing attackers.

A dog being taught to hold an object, a folded newspaper in this case. Photo by Louise Van Der Meid.

FETCH

Fetching or retrieving a thrown object comes naturally to some dogs. Dropping a fetched object at your feet, however, has to be taught. Dogs working as trackers and searchers must first be proficient in fetching. Many dogs will drop a retrieved object at the feet of their masters. Some do not. These can be taught to hold the retrieved object until commanded to drop it. Holding onto an aggressor, of course, is a desirable "trick."

Bulldogs, by the way, having been bred for bull-baiting, hold on vice-like when they seize a bull by the snout. The bulldog's stance and low center of gravity keep it from being thrown too easily by an enraged steer. The respiratory function of its receding nose is hardly hampered even when blood gushes down into its face from an injured bull. The bulldog holds tight. Hence the expression "holds on like a bulldog."

Front (top) and rear (bottom) of commercial kennels. Note the convenient access to the rear of each dog's quarters. Photos courtesy of Security Dogs, Hialeah, Florida.

The face value of deterrent force. Photo courtesy of Security Dogs, Hialeah, Florida.

Potential intruders don't want to be at the business end of a German Shepherd's teeth.

Learning to bark when someone approaches the car.

HOLD

If the dog insists on dropping the fetched object at your feet when you are not ready for it, gently hold the dog's jaws together, saying *HOLD*. A second or two, no more, is enough, otherwise you may discourage the dog from fetching. (Roughness in shoving articles into the dog's mouth and yanking them out can cause a dog to chomp down hard on what it retrieves and to chew it up.) The dog should continue to hold after you release the pressure. If not, reprimand by voice, replace the object in the dog's mouth and repeat until what you want is understood.

SPEAK

Any dog worth its keep knows when to bark (and some do not know when to stop). When your dog barks, try to use the opportunity to have it associate the comment *SPEAK* with the bark.

GO [GET IT]

When the foregoing commands have been learned, you may teach the dog to take off in a direction you point out.

Leave your dog in a sitting position and walk about one hundred feet away, remaining within the dog's sight. When you know the dog is watching you, pretend to put something on the ground in front of you. Return to your dog. Give the command GO, point to the spot where you pretended to put something. When your dog just approaches that spot, command *LIE DOWN*. Go to your dog and praise it. Return to where the dog started, and command your dog to *COME*.

Learning to GO GET IT!

The large size and the big voice of a Great Dane are enough to discourage loiterers and snoopers about the house. Photo by Dr. H.R. Axelrod.

German Shepherds learning to control their bite. Note the effect of dog teeth on the padding. Photos courtesy of Security Dogs, Hialeah, Florida.

A trio of Labradors poised to retrieve the quarry. Getting used to gunfire is an important element in the training of hunting dogs. Photo courtesy of Winchester-Western Division, Olin Mathieson Chemical Corporation.

GUNFIRE

As with sporting dogs, protection dogs must not be gun-shy.

Gradually decrease (over days or weeks) the distance between someone firing a small caliber gun or pistol and your dog who is pleasantly engaged in eating; this is a way to help the dog associate gunfire with pleasantness.

Another way is to have an associate fire a weapon, preferably a .22 caliber one, at about 300 feet while you are walking your dog on a leash. Watch your dog carefully. Quickly assuage (by petting and consoling) any apprehension it may show toward the report of the weapon.

DEVELOPING AGILITY

Know the limitations of your breed. Maximize the natural ability of your own dog. Forcing your dog beyond these limitations and abilities can ruin the animal.

To jump obstacles, the dog is taught as follows.

Command *UP* and encourage the dog to jump over low hurdles (low means low enough for you). If you do this with the dog on a leash, do not hamper the dog's jump by putting any tension on the leash. Lead the dog to the center of the hurdle so that it does not circumvent the obstacle. Try to synchronize the command *UP* with the instant the dog starts its leap. When your dog knows what is expected, you can stop going along during the jump.

Jumping exercises can be pleasant as play for most dogs. Other types of hurdles can be improvised from a variety of articles normally found in the home.

Making friends. Note the absence of padded jacket on the trainer. Photo courtesy of Security Dogs, Hialeah, Florida.

"Warning, BAD DOG" signs being loaded at an airport. Such warning signs do have an effect regardless of the actual presence (or absence) of any dogs at all. Photo courtesy of Security Dogs, Hialeah, Florida.

The size of the Shepherd guard dog's paw is easily seen and compared with the hand of the trainer in this picture. Notice the padding under the trainer's jacket. Eighty to ninety pounds of lunging dog behind paws of this size are formidable enough even without teeth. Photo courtesy of Security Dogs, Hialeah, Florida.

German Shepherd on a scent track along a fence over which an "escapee" climbed shortly before this picture was taken. Photo courtesy of Security Dogs, Hialeah, Florida.

Gradually teach the dog (and yourself) how to recognize broader jumps; move each of a series of hurdles further and further apart until both you and your dog realize that further distance is too much to ask. (There may be exceptional circumstances, of course, where a dog can make super-dog efforts, but do not train for that.)

To scale an obstacle too high to jump, command *UP AND OVER*. Begin low and build up height. Avoid very high obstacles because a dog still has to come down even after it successfully gets up and over! (Cats do better in landings.) When a dog scales well, have it learn to stay put after landing, and teach it to return over the hurdle to you.

Learning to ROLL OVER. This is easier with some bitches who have a tendency, anyway, to roll over, apparently to be scratched on the abdomen. This behavior may be a gesture of submission to their human masters, or even to stronger, more dominating dogs.

SHAKE is a popular and expressive trick, enabling the dog to aptly "speak" without barking. When an owner tries to ignore a dog's wistful gaze, a big and plushy uplifted paw can gain immediate favorable response when begging for a tidbit, to go out, or for almost anything. Non-aggressive "tricks" like SHAKE, or ROLL OVER are usually part of every dog's bag of tricks. And these can be more easily demonstrated to visiting friends and relatives than can the protective maneuvers which hurdle 50 to 90 pounds of dog through the air toward the guests.

DOG VERSUS BULLET

The following thought should be kept in mind as we go into more aggressive phases of protection; even though an eighty-pound dog is a fearsome weapon, it can be recalled . . . unlike the bullet, which halts only in its target. Yet, many a criminal prefers the bullet to the dog.

In spite of its savage ancestry, the Siberian Husky is known to be a gentle, faithful dog. Photo by Dr. H.R. Axelrod.

A rampant German Shepherd guard dog stands high enough for eyeball-to-eyeball contact with a crouching housebreaker. Photo courtesy of Security Dogs, Hialeah, Florida.

Encouraging the trainee to get a good hold on the "assailant." Photo courtesy of Security Dogs, Hialeah, Florida.

AGGRESSIVE PHASES OF PROTECTION

You must have full control of your dog as it develops its more offensive qualities. The dog is encouraged to have a dual personality; it has to carry out protective duties when confronted with strangers, but should be friendly toward family and friends. What is desired, in effect, is instant hostility (but not viciousness) on command, with reversion to docility after the immediate problem is resolved. Continual hostility is unwanted and unwarranted.

For training adult dogs, you must use protective clothing, that is, padded suits or at least a padded or reinforced arm covering for a dog to seize upon. Such protective clothing, however, makes an unnatural-looking aggressor.

Young dogs may tend to associate padding with seizing and holding, thus may only go after aggressors who happen to look like they are wearing training suits!

The person playing the part of the aggressor must be quite knowledgeable and proficient in such work. The proper attitude of your dog towards an aggressor is affected by this person's skill.

Pursuit and seizure lessons are described below. *STOP HIM* is the key command here.

STOP HIM – PRELIMINARY GRIPPING STAGE

Teach your dog to take hold of and pull on a strip of tough fabric. Pull the dog several steps, increasing tension on the fabric strip; the dog should tighten its grip when you pull like that. Praise the dog amply.

Learning to hold on to an assailant. Note that in later lessons the padding is concealed under the jacket to present a more natural appearance to the dog. Otherwise he might learn to attack only people who wear padded arm protectors! Photo courtesy of Security Dogs, Hialeah, Florida.

The muzzle is used when transporting several aggressive dogs together, thus preventing casualties. Photo courtesy of Security Dogs, Hialeah, Florida.

Agitation of a trainee Shepherd preceding actual training. Photo courtesy of Security Dogs, Hialeah, Florida.

To avoid possible deaths from motor accidents, it is imperative that dogs, particularly small ones like a Dachshund, must be trained not to venture into the street with traffic or chase moving vehicles. Photo by Al Berry of Three Lions, Inc.

Training session with padded arm. Photo courtesy of Security Dog, Hialeah, Florida.

LEAVE [OFF]

Be certain to teach the dog to release the cloth instantaneously the moment you command *LEAVE*. Having your dog fully comply with this essential command depends not only upon your skill in conveying to the dog the difference between what is expected from it doing fetching, holding and tugging exercises, but also depends upon your dog. Some dogs, let's face it, are not born to be ideal protection dogs. Any dog, however, which has progressed beyond basic obedience training can be taught enough to make it a useful animal, more or less.

In initial exercises with a padded arm, the dog must be coaxed to respond to the provocation and to take hold. Photo courtesy of Security Dogs, Hialeah, Florida.

Doberman on guard duty. . . on leash. Photo
courtesy of Security Dogs, Hialeah, Florida.

STOP HIM –
ADVANCED GRIPPING STAGE

Once a dog tugs adequately at the fabric, holding and releasing it on command, wrap it loosely around your (or your assistant's) forearm. Then, with a minimum of agitation and excitement, encourage your dog to seize the strip of fabric. Gradually, as the dog learns, leave less and less of the fabric hanging loose, thus concentrating the dog's attention on the sleeve itself.

STOP HIM – PURSUIT STAGE

Have the dog sit at your side. Your assistant approaches and begins speaking with you, and slowly lopes away. Wait a moment to avoid your dog's anticipating your command, then say *STOP HIM!* As in the hurdling exercises earlier in this book, go along with your dog. It should be on the leash during these first trials.

At first, your assistant "assailant" may even have to hold out his arm to encourage the dog to seize it.

Some trainers elect to have a dog release the moment resistance ceases; others train their dogs to release on command.

If, after the fabric stimulus is eliminated, the dog does not respond properly, go back to a point at which the dog did well, and build back up again to the proper response.

Dry runs are essential so that the dog is not expected to seize an assailant during each and every chase.

In police work, the dog is trained to end his active role as soon as the policeman-handler questions or searches the fugitive. It's function is then to stand by, ready and alert, between the fugitive and the policeman-handler. The policeman-handler, when finished, calls the dog to his side and they both accompany the "prisoner" back to where they are going. Note, however, that when the "fugitive" is not arrested, the dog must understand that his hostile role is over, and that the "fugitive" is allowed to leave. On the other hand, note also that some dogs are trained to attack on their own initiative when their policeman-handler is knocked down.

Dog trainer teaching the dog to charge an armed assailant. Photo courtesy of Security Dogs, Hialeah, Florida.

The dog is trained to subdue an assailant regardless of any threats posed by such a person. Photo courtesy of Security Dogs, Hialeah, Florida.

Here the dog easily circumvents an assailant's whip. (The dog and trainer in this picture are really good friends! A dog in training is quite aware of the meaning of practice enemies and real ones.) Photo courtesy of Security Dogs, Hialeah, Florida.

STOP HIM/WATCH HIM—AT BAY

Here, the dog is trained to pursue and hold the fugitive at bay while barking, but without seizing the fugitive. This exercise trains a dog to safely stand off someone who has a striking weapon (crowbar, stick, etc.). The dog is not allowed to approach the fugitive too closely nor to take hold of him, but is trained to circle the man and keep on barking. The man playing the fugitive also turns around, facing the dog as it circles about. To avoid entanglements, the leash can be left off in this exercise.

The "fugitive" later runs away but stops short before the dog seizes him. The man can use a club or stick to discourage the dog from attempting a hold. The man playing the fugitive, however, should be careful not to hurt the dog in this exercise.

Dogs are also trained to pursue under gunfire. In addition to what was said about this training earlier in this book, one may also train a younger dog in the presence of an older, experienced dog. The inexperienced dog who hesitates under fire will probably soon be eager to participate once it watches the older dog go through its paces.

PRECAUTION

Dry runs, we repeat, are essential to train the dog to pursue and hold only upon command, and not to respond merely to all running people or to a man who (innocently enough) may be carrying a walking stick or golf club.

ESCAPEES

When a dog learns to escort a prisoner back, in the company of its policeman-handler, check on the dog's alertness by having your "prisoner" assistant pretend to escape custody. Then present the dog with the real escape by your "prisoner." Do not exercise these little extras too often, however, for the dog could be overly suspicious and hostile.

PERSONAL PROTECTION

Personal protection duties of a dog include guarding a house, car, baby in a stroller or carriage, an elderly person or an invalid in a wheelchair, or the cashier in a family business (restaurant, garage or filling station, food stands, stores, etc.). Personal protection is also afforded by the dog who accompanies its master or mistress on walks.

One should train the right dog for the right job, that is, the right *breed* and the right *individual* of that breed. A boat or fishing enthusiast who wants to boat or fish in the company of a dog would do well in choosing a natural swimmer, although many other breeds of dogs can swim well.

Training a dog for personal protection is, in effect, a synthesis of all the training steps described throughout this whole book. Select just what elements of advanced training you need for your own purposes.

A series of photographs in the section dealing with the Canine Detail of the Miami Police Department depict steps in the training of a German Shepherd to protect its owner from the simulated purse-snatcher (both owner or handler and fugitive are policemen). The old adage, "The best defense is a good offense" should not always be taken too seriously. In most cases, however, protection training is best restricted to merely *looking* aggressive and perhaps growling aggressively, but being, above all, *obedient*. If you cannot call the dog off an attacker, then forget the whole idea of a protection dog, for it will become your greatest liability. (Notice that we do not say *would-be* attacker because the dog owner who unleashes a dangerous animal had better be dead certain that the supposed attacker is really intent on attacking!)

Obtaining a suitable dog is the first step in raising a protection dog. Dog size may be a powerful deterrent to anyone considering stealing from or attacking a person with a dog. Yet the Chihuahua, for example, has been known to be the meanest loudmouth who ever bit the ankle of an intruder. A Chihuahua will hardly kill anyone (unless from rabies or tetanus!), yet will certainly adequately alarm an owner soon enough of any out-of-the-ordinary events.

Chihuahuas are well known "alarmists" in the dog world. In spite of their puny size these dogs will try to protect their owners. Photo courtesy of Three Lions.

Protection training is really ordinary dog training—such as that presented in this book—applied to the specific purpose of having the dog (1) sit or stand when told, and not move until told to do so, or given a pre-arranged sign to come, or to go fetch help, and (2) bark or growl (that is, "speaking") on command or at a given sign (such as anyone who raises a stick at it or its owner). Some protective maneuvers are instinctive to dogs, and require only that the owner encourage—that is, reinforce—them once they are discovered. For example, a loyal dog usually interposes itself between its owner and any suspicious-looking (to the dog) or unknown person. The owner's only concern here is to train the dog not to leap up on that unknown person.

Emphasize, from among the "tricks" described throughout this book, just those aggressive ones needed for a particular dog's own private training. Teach growling (but only growling) upon the approach of strangers at odd times or places. Showing the teeth, too, is quite a forceful warning sign. A way to teach these two warning actions is to capitalize upon every occasion when your dog naturally growls or bares its teeth. Reward or chastise every growl or gnashing of the teeth, depending upon whether you wish to encourage or discourage such a response to a given stimulus. That is, chastise for showing a mouthful of teeth to your mother-in-law, but reward for a warning bark at anyone prowling across your porch at 1 a.m. . . . not 5 a.m., for that is probably the milkman!

Again, protection is, in many cases, merely the presence of an obedient dog. Protection training is therefore basic dog training plus a few aggressive (or aggressive-looking, preferably) actions. Perusal of this book will help you to understand the psyche of the dog, its basic training, possibilities for its advanced training, and how to develop your dog's natural traits—breed traits and individual traits—best suited for your needs.

Protection, then, can be merely *looks*, or it can be a ferocious (but recallable) lunge. Never forget (and the neighbors and the law will never let you forget) that each progressively more dangerous "trick" your dog learns, the more progressively proficient *you* must become in controlling your dog.

THE MIAMI
POLICE DEPARTMENT
CANINE DETAIL*

The Miami (Florida) Police Department organized their canine detail to take advantage of dogs' excellent senses of smell and hearing, enabling them to search out and detect a hidden person much more quickly than can usually be done by a human being. They also are good for seeking evidence dropped by a perpetrator of a crime. A dog's nose detects odors in the air that cannot be detected by quite sensitive chemical tests.

Dogs overtake fleeing persons much more rapidly and readily than human runners.

Dogs protect policemen not only in discovering persons, but in preventing and repulsing attacks.

Dogs are capable of holding an offender while the police-man handler searches a second person or goes to summon assistance.

Dogs are useful in quelling riots and disorderly crowds, particularly because most people fear large dogs.

Under the proper circumstances, dogs can track escaping offenders, prowlers, peeping toms, or lost persons.

Police dogs do not solve all problems. Their effectiveness depends upon intelligent application of their capabilities. The misuse of dogs wastes police time and effort and confuses the dogs, requiring retraining, if indeed they are not ruined for further use.

In addition to policemen-handler teams being assigned to the radio patrol task force, these teams are available at any time to any other police unit.

* This chapter is based upon a Miami Police Deparment fact sheet kindly made available by Sgt. William G. Nelson and Officer Calvin Ross.

Section of Miami Police Department Canine Detail at a public performance. Miami Police Department photo by R.W. Johnson.

LOGISTICS

City of Miami Police Dogs (male German Shepherds, 12 to 36 months old) are donated by citizens. The cost to the city for maintaining a dog is minimal—about 1/20th to 1/25th the salary of a policeman.

The dogs are fed once a day, usually after their tour of duty, with one pound of beef, two pounds of dry feed and one vitamin capsule. A heartworm preventive agent and a skin and coat conditioner are added to the food. These dogs are issued a doghouse, a sixteen-foot lead, one short lead for use in traffic, one tracking harness, one twenty-five-foot tracking lead, one feed pan, one water bucket, one grooming brush, one comb, one choke chain collar and one attack collar.

SPECIFIC EMPLOYMENT OF DOGS

Although dogs are trained not to attack a man in uniform, the plainclothes personnel at a crime scene are encouraged to report to the field sergeant in charge of the uniformed personnel answering the call; the plainclothesmen are advised not to enter a building being searched by dogs until the policemen-handlers are aware of the additional people on the scene. The dog protects his policeman-handler at all times. The dog may even view a friendly slap on his handler's back as a threat. Shaking hands, too, with the dog's handler should be done cautiously!

If the dog is free and holding a suspect at bay, plainclothesmen are advised not to attempt to frisk the suspect or to take over at the scene until the handler regains control of his dog.

Dogs are limited as to the types of duty and the areas where they are most effective. They are assigned, in general, to areas where the breaking-and-entering rate is high, usually 7:00 p.m. to 3:00 a.m., but are subject to call 24 hours a day. Teams are assigned to foot patrols in areas with high crime rates. The number of crimes against persons (particularly purse snatchers and strongarm robberies) appears to have decreased where dogs are assigned to beats.

PHYSICAL AND MENTAL ATTRIBUTES OF THE POLICEMAN-HANDLER AND HIS DOG

When a dog is offered to the Miami Police Department, he is examined by the instructor for general conformation to the average German Shepherd standard. The dog must not be too aggressive nor too timid. After a veterinarian examines a dog medically, he is tested for gunshyness. When a dog passes these tests, he is assigned to a policeman-handler. Both this handler and the dog start training together.

The policeman-handler must have been in the police department for two years and have a good record. He must own fenced-in property. His family and neighbors must consent to his living day and night with the dog. He must understand and like animals because he is responsible for the dog twenty-four hours a day, including the animal's health, grooming and feeding. The policeman-handler teaches the dog to have a dual personality: to be a friendly household pet when at home and a hard-hitting attack dog when field conditions require.

ACTUAL TRAINING

The twelve-week course, based on the training course used by the City of London (England) Police Department, is divided into four phases: familiarization and obedience, tracking, attack, and search.

The obedience and attack phases are covered elsewhere in this book. Hand signals are also taught for each command in those phases as well as for the phases which follow, although these signals are seldom used on actual duty.

TRACKING

Tracking is used in following and apprehending a suspect fleeing the scene of a crime. The dog is accustomed to

Training sequence of a purse snatcher being stopped by a dog. Miami Police Department photos by R.W. Johnson. Above, a purse snatcher (actually a policeman) approaches his victim (another policeman) and the dog, hidden in the carriage. Below, the snatch is made, and the purse snatcher begins to bolt away. Notice the protective arm covering worn by the purse snatcher.

The victim orders the dog out of the carriage and after the criminal.

Having almost caught up with the purse snatcher, the dog prepares to grab him until its trainer (the victim) catches up.

The dog has grabbed onto the criminal and is holding on until the trainer reaches the scene of the action and gives the appropriate command.

A dog learning to jump on command. Note the platform to break the dog's descent. This minimizes training accidents as well as accustoms the dog to landing on a floor after leaping through a window or other opening. Also, the platform can be used to train the dog to jump from a higher to a lower spot, such as leaving the upper storey of a building, or jumping down into a cellar. Miami Police Department photo by R.W. Johnson.

wearing a tracking (chest) harness and being attached to a twenty-five foot tracking lead, giving him greater freedom of movement than the usual six-food lead gives.

The dog learns to follow a twenty-five foot track laid a few seconds before. The trainer gradually increases the length of the track and the time of the run until the dog can follow an hour-old, mile-long track. The policeman-handlers lay tracks for each other's dogs. As the dog learns to track, he also learns to find and indicate to his handler any articles dropped by the suspect along the track. The command used in this training is a softly spoken *SEEK*.

While combing wooded areas, no surprises can drop out of a tree or pop up from behind a bush when man and dog search as a team. Miami Police Department photo by R.W. Johnson.

Tracking involves a dog's detecting and following a ground scent until the person or object which left the scent is found. Scent depends upon many factors: the person being tracked and the environment; the person's health and state of nutrition, mental state, hygiene, sex and race affect his or her scent, as well as the part of the body leaving the scent. Mechanics, bakers, chemical workers, physicians, etc., all have their distinctive scent to dogs. Wool, linen, synthetics, leather, rubber in clothing and shoes all have distinctive scents. Plowed soil, crushed insects and grass, flowers, also have distinctive scents.

Weather affects the success of tracking operations. Traffic—foot or vehicular—obliterates a track of scent very rapidly. Heat, strong wind and rain wipe out a track. Mild weather, however, especially when ground temperature is greater than air temperature, aids the dog in following his track.

SEARCH

A dog learns to search buildings, room by room, floor by floor, and to overcome obstacles, scale walls, go through windows and so on. The dog also learns to search woods and other places encountered on duty.

The odor in a building locked up for the night dissipates. A burglar brings fresh, strong odor of his own, usually accentuated by his own nervousness. This fresh odor pervades the immediate area around the burglar and along his track inside of the building.

A policeman who suspects an unauthorized entry in a building summons help to surround it and should also call for a canine team. The policeman-handler opens the door for his dog and immediately closes the door after the dog enters, thus minimizing drafts which tend to dissipate the telltale odor of the burglar. The dog, familiar with the smell of his own handler, is attracted to the only other strong odor—that of the suspect.

A dog relies upon airborne scent in searching. Searching also requires a dog's policeman-handler to be observant of all signs made by his dog. The dog is taught to *quietly* locate and point out a person, and then to bark.

THE WHOLE PICTURE

All parts of a canine program are equally important because a combination of all of these parts will be utilized in actual operations (riots, dispersing an unruly crowd, etc.). The mere presence of a dog is sometimes enough to disperse a crowd; dogs are kept on a leash in crowd situations for obvious reasons.

THE CANINE CAR

Each canine team—one dog and one policeman-handler—is assigned a special car, the rear of which is fitted with a kennel and a bucket always kept filled with clean, cool water.

ARE POLICE DOGS DANGEROUS?

The Miami Police Department immediately accepts invitations to demonstrate their dogs and what they can do for any group, school or club. In these demonstrations, they point out the friendliness and obedience of their dogs. Children are allowed to pet the dogs. This approach was felt to convince the public that a police dog is not a vicious animal to be feared needlessly at all times. And, in fact, their tactful use of the dogs on assignments has brought compliments from the public and the news media. There is no doubt that public knowledge of the presence and capabilities of these dogs has resulted in more control over crime in many areas.

THE NARCOTICS DOG*

Dogs can detect very small concentrations of scent. Experiments revealed that a dog's olfactory acuity is one million times better than that of man. A dog can be trained to detect one teaspoon of salt in thirteen gallons of water, one teaspoon of acetic acid (the acid in vinegar) diluted with thirteen hundred gallons of pure water (that is, a ratio

---

* Based upon a fact sheet by Sgt. Harold Whitaker, Canine Detail, Miami Police Department.

The buddy system—police officer and police dog look out for one another 24 hours a day. Miami Police Department photo by R.W. Johnson.

of one part acid to one million parts water), one part sulfuric acid in ten million parts of water, and one part urine masked with sixty million parts of pure water. Dogs can differentiate between artifical musk and the natural animal product, two products quite indistinguishable to human beings.

Trained dogs are capable of analyzing complex mixtures of odors. Nitrobenzol, mixed with four or five other substances, can still be detected by a dog, but not by human beings. This analytical ability to distinguish mixed and masked odors is utilized in training a dog to search for narcotics.

Although any basically trained dog who enjoys nose work (that is, searching for articles, tracking, etc.) might be trained to seek narcotics, trained utility police dogs, however, have been taught man work, that is, protecting their policemen-handlers and attacking aggressors, and have learned to become aggressive when a suspect is found during a building search. If such a dog must be used in narcotics work, care should be taken in retraining the dog to eliminate aggressive behavior from this activity of seeking narcotics. Preferably, the dog should be selected from the beginning as a specialist and trained only for this kind of nose work.

German Shepherds have been used successfully in narcotics, but their natural alertness (to unusual noises for example) could distract them while searching for drugs. Highstrung or easily distracted dogs would have a difficult time of it working around noisy machinery or airports. Bloodhounds are over-rated!

The Labrador Retriever is a willing worker, responds well to training, has excellent scenting ability and has a sensible disposition. Labs are curious but not easily distracted.

A bitch is not as easily distracted as a male dog is by other dog odors, but she is usually smaller than the male.

DISEASES

Your dog may pick up external or internal parasites. External parasites are fleas, lice, ticks and mange mites. Internal parasites include roundworms, tapeworms, flukes (trematodes) and protozoa.

Infectious diseases which a dog may acquire include distemper, leptospirosis, tularemia, nocardosis, and histoplasmosis.

Other than reference to *The Dog Owner's Encyclopedia of Veterinary Medicine* and advice to consult your veterinarian, the treatment of many of the conditions noted in this section will not be discussed in detail. As always, good care and maintenance is the best course.

Mange—caused by several kinds of mites—is prevented by good grooming and diet, clean and dry bedding and quarters, and freedom from internal parasites. Note, however, that most creatures, you, I *and* the dog—have *some* internal parasites. A debilitating population of parasites is what we must watch for in our dogs.

Other skin conditions are caused by fungus (includes the so-called "ringworm" infection), bacteria (pyoderma, caused by *Staphylococcus*, etc.), allergy (due to insect bites, foods, drugs), hormonal imbalance, and sebaceous gland overactivity (seborrhea). The cause of summer eczema (also called summer dermatitis or seasonal dermatitis) is not fully agreed upon.

Ticks are a common nuisance to outdoor living dogs, especially hunting dogs or those which run through fields and woods. Ticks attach to the dog's skin and cause irritation. Engorged ticks may grow to the size of a quarter; this becomes a problem when the site of attachment is deep in the dog's ear. If a tick is pulled out but its head left embedded in the dog's skin, infection may occur around it. Do not try to pick out a head that stays in. Just expect a little pustule to form. Apply antiseptic to it.

Remove a tick by grasping it close to the skin (using forceps or your fingers) and exerting a steady pull until it comes out with its head still on. Apply an antiseptic.

The brown tick of dogs may carry a protozoan infection, piroplasmosis, particularly in Florida and other tropical areas. The American dog tick and Rocky Mountain spotted tick can cause paralysis.

The brown tick adapts well to pestering dogs in their kennels and heated homes, as well as in yards of homes in the southern states. Ticks do not live long in cold weather and dry, unheated buildings, but winter in the southern states may not be severe enough to kill off ticks on dogs which live outdoors.

Fleas (except the sticktight species) migrate freely over the dog, so that liquid or powder treatment (on back, head and neck only) or dog flea collars are generally effective if the fleas are given time to roam through the treated areas.

Sticktight fleas must be doused directly with chemicals. A multitude of flea sprays, powders and other preparations are available for removing and protecting against these insects.

Fleas can transmit tapeworm or heartworm. Some animals are allergic to flea saliva and develop dermatitis where bitten by the fleas.

"Worms" include many varieties of parasitic roundworms and flatworms, the most common of which are ascarids (large, intestinal roundworms), heartworms, hookworms and tapeworms. Only one species of fluke—the salmon-poisoning fluke—is a problem; it occurs in the northwestern states and southwestern Canada. The salmon-poisoning fluke transmits a rickettsia-like organism which causes salmon poisoning. Raw or improperly cooked fish of the salmon family are responsible for harboring this disease.

Ascarids and tapeworms are visible to the naked eye. Ascarids look like dirty pink or white glistening fragments of spaghetti, and can be recovered from vomitus and sometimes from feces. Tapeworm fragments look like slightly transparent ribbons.

FIRST AID

A severely injured dog may be so blinded by pain that it even attempts to bite its master. If necessary, make a muzzle from a strip of cloth or bandage by wrapping it around (crossing it under the jaws) and tying it behind the ears, on the top of the head.

Injury and illness may be quite obvious, or may require close scrutiny to locate. Wounds may be from automobile accidents, cuts from glass, sharp objects, wire, bites from other animals, puncture wounds, and foreign objects (thorns, glass splinters, tacks, etc.)

The emergency care suggested below is based upon recommendations by a veterinarian*.

In automobile accidents where the dog is apparently affected, you may have to treat for shock. This is done by covering the dog with a blanket and allowing him to rest. Console him with voice and hand, keeping him quiet and in a darkened area. Internal injury is sometimes indicated by white gums. When it is obvious that the dog must be seen by a veterinarian—such as when a dog is unconscious —wrap a bandage tightly around the body so as to form a sheath. Keep the dog very quiet until the veterinarian arrives.

For bee stings give an antihistamine cold tablet and apply cold compresses over the area of the sting. A veterinarian should be called if there is any question as to the effect of the sting on the dog.

For bites from other animals, shave the area which has been bitten and apply an antiseptic solution by flowing it into puncture wounds with an eyedropper. Ordinary household antiseptics such as Merthiolate or iodine can be used. In cases of obviously bad bites, when a dog has been

* If the dog will not swallow, place two tablespoons of salt on the back of his tongue and close his mouth.

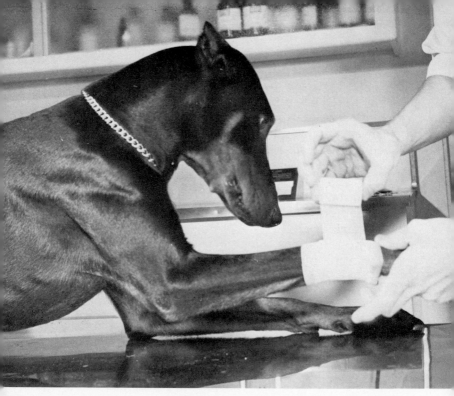

The injured foreleg of a Doberman being fixed by a veterinarian.

badly torn up, take him to your veterinarian. If ordinary superficial wounds become infected after you have treated them, you should also see your veterinarian.

Apply cold water to burns. Water-immersible creams can be used in the dressings afterwards. Consult the veterinarian immediately unless the burn is quite minor.

For broken legs, immobilize the broken limb with a splint. The whole dog should be immobilized if other bones (ribs, pelvis, back, shoulder) are fractured. Call the veterinarian immediately.

Choking on foreign objects (bones, wood, etc.) may be alleviated by removing the object—if it can be seen at the back of the mouth or the thoat. If the object cannot be removed because it's either too far back in the throat or is too deeply imbedded in the tissue, rush your dog to the veterinarian immediately.

Cuts and lacerations, when they are very minor, are treated adequately by the dog's licking them. If the dog cannot reach his minor cuts, you may clean them with hydrogen peroxide (make certain that the solution is fresh, otherwise all the oxygen would have escaped!), then apply a household antiseptic such as Merthiolate. For severe cuts and lacerations, apply a pressure bandage (that is, a compress that you hold or tie on with pressure being applied) to control hemorrhage. Minor cuts which become infected sometime after you treat them should also be seen by a veterinarian.

For dislocations, keep the dog quiet and take him to a veterinarian immediately.

When a drowning dog has been retrieved, apply artificial respiration as follows: lay the dog on his side, push with your hand on his ribs, and release quickly. Repeat the maneuver every three seconds. Treat the dog for shock as described above under automobile accident.

Artificial respiration is also applied to a dog which has received a stunning electric shock. Treat for shock in this case also. The veterinarian should be consulted immediately.

Rapidly immerse a dog which has succumbed to heat stroke in cold water until it is obvious that the dog has some relief. Lay the dog flat and pour cold water over him and then turn the electric fan over him adding more cold water as it evaporates. Be careful, however, not to mix the water with the electricity, thus endangering both the dog and his helper! Press cold towels against the dog's abdomen and the back of his head in order to reduce temperature quickly if a quantity of cold water is not available for pouring over him. Avoid cooling the dog so much that you chill him. Some authorities, in fact, advise against using cold water. Call a veterinarian immediately.

A dog who has been stuck with porcupine quills is in bad shape. Tie the dog up or hold him securely between your knees. Use pliers to pull out all of the quills. Do not forget the inside of the mouth. A veterinarian may be consulted to remove the quills which are too deeply imbedded for you to extract.

For poisonous snake bites, cut a deep (quarter-inch) X over the fang marks. Drip potassium permanganate or fresh hydrogen peroxide into the wound. Apply a tourniquet above the bite if it is on a foot or leg. This first aid should be given only if a veterinarian or physician cannot be reached.

When your dog has been poisoned, or you believe your suspicion is strongly warranted, remember that prompt action is essential. A general emetic for use when the kind of poison is unknown can be made from hydrogen peroxide and water, and the second is merely a sudsy solution of soap and water. Force the dog to swallow up to twelve tablespoons of one of these mixtures (a 50 to 70 lb. dog), or six tablespoons for a 20 to 30 lb. dog, or two to three tablespoons for a five to ten pound dog. The dog will regurgitate the contents of his stomach within a few minutes. If the dog will not swallow, place two tablespoons of salt on the back of his tongue and close his mouth. Call your veterinarian immediately. Try to find the container from which the poison came, if possible, so that the antidote on the label may be followed.

It is important to remember that the following symptoms of poisoning may also occur in other conditions, but under certain circumstances when poisoning is suspected, they may also apply to a poisoned dog: trembling, panting, intestinal pain, vomiting, slimy secretion from the mouth, convulsions and coma.

Dogs, particularly younger animals who are not as used to traveling as older ones, may get car-sick. If the dog is afraid for some reason, this may also contribute to his car-sickness.

Begin to accustom your dog to the car by giving it short and frequent trips, cutting down on food and water several hours before riding.

CANINE HONOR ROLL—TRIBUTES TO DOGS

Although there are too many stories of dogs—their services to mankind and their love for their masters—to retell here or to even retell at all, the following tributes (partly by name, partly as a general tribute to unknown canine soldiers) give some notion of the extent of dogs in action for their masters, and indirectly for us all.

TROOPER—A POLICE DOG

This seventy-five pound German Shepherd was on patrol with Officer Vernon Scoville of the Kansas City Police Department just before dawn on March 17, 1961 when two men in an alley attacked the officer.

One of the men—300 lbs. and over six feet—seized Scoville's flashlight and struck the officer over the head with it. The other man beat Trooper on the back with a tire wrench as the dog flew at the larger of the two assailants. Scoville, injured and bleeding but relieved momentarily from attack as his dog tore into the big assailant, was able to pull his revolver out of its holster and shoot. The surviving assailant attempted to escape in his car, but stopped and surrendered after Scoville ordered Trooper to *"get him."*

With Trooper standing guard, Officer Scoville made his way out of the alley where he found a citizen to telephone for assistance.

Officer Scoville's wife was the only person who was

able to coax Trooper from the patrol car which took Scoville to the hospital.

Trooper had taken a beating, too, and his hindquarters became progressively more paralyzed until he had to be put out of his misery. He now lies buried in the Canine Corps Training Ground, Kansas City.

AND MANY OTHER DOGS

Nameless are the legions of savage battle dogs employed by ancient armies. As time went on, however, the numbers of dogs used in battle decreased, although the Spanish King Carlos V used numbers of war dogs (donated by King Henry VIII of England), and Napoleon reinforced his Egyptian positions with masses of dogs as sentries.

The Russians employed dogs during the Russo-Japanese War to seek out wounded soldiers.

During the First World War, dogs carried mess tins to German outposts, and Belgian troops employed dogs to haul ammunition and machine guns, just as the Italians set thier alpine farm dogs to pull machine guns along mountain trails during the Second World War.

In World War II, dogs were trained to noiselessly notify their handlers of the presence of strangers (the enemy, that is), seek out snipers, sniff out mines, especially when plastic mines were missed by more sophisticated mine detectors, search out booby trap trip wires, carry messages between battle-beseiged units, and jump with commandos.

Ricky, a Welsh sheepdog, detected mines along a canal in the Netherlands, was wounded by one of them which exploded, but was so well trained and had such a personality, that he carried on without panicking.

A dog named Chips guarded Roosevelt and Churchill at a 1943 conference, and, during operations in North Africa and Sicily, Chips charged a machine gun nest.

Silver, of the U.S. Fifth Army, detected hardly audible (to human ears) sounds of German infantrymen fixing bayonets in preparation for a surprise charge against U.S. positions in Italy.

Rex searched for injured people trapped in burning buildings in England during World War II.

DOGS AND THE SENATOR FROM MISSOURI

Senator Vest of Missouri, pleading for the plaintiff whose dog had been shot in malice:

"Gentlemen of the jury: . . . the people who are prone to fall on their knees to do us honor when success is with us may be the first to throw the stone of malice when failure settles its clouds upon our heads.

"The one absolutely unselfish friend that man can have in this selfish world, the one that never deserts him, the one that never proves ungrateful or treacherous, is his dog. A man's dog stands by him in prosperity and poverty, in health and sickness. He will sleep on the cold ground, when the wintry winds blow and the snow drives fiercely, if only he may be near his master's side. He will kiss the hand that has no food to offer; he will lick the wound and sores that come in encounter with roughness of the world. He guards the sleep of his pauper master as if he were a prince. When all other friends desert, he remains. When riches take wings and reputation falls to pieces, he is as constant in his love as the sun in its journey through the heavens.

"If fortune drives the master forth, an outcast in the world, friendless and homeless, the faithful dog asks no higher privilege than that of accompanying him, to guard against danger, to fight his enemies; and when the last scene of all comes, and death takes the master in its embrace, and his body is laid away in the cold ground, no matter if all other friends pursue their way, there by the graveside will the noble dog be found, his head between his paws, his eyes sad, but open in watchfulness, faithful and true, even in death."

The jury returned a verdict in favor of the plaintiff for two and one-half times the amount for which he was suing ($500.00 awarded instead of $200.00 because of the effect of Senator Vest's eulogy before the jury).

FINAL THOUGHTS ON THE DOG—
FRIEND OF THY HEART

Over a hundred years ago, a wandering naturalist (Goodrich, 1859) quoted another traveler (Burchell, *Travels in Africa*) on the fidelity and value of the dog, man's best friend:

> *"We felt a confidence that no danger could approach us at night without being announced by their barking. . . often, in the middle of the night, when all my people have been fast asleep around the fire, have I stood to contemplate these faithful animals lying by their side, and have learned to esteem them for their social esteem of mankind. When wandering over pathless deserts, oppressed with vexation and distress at the conduct of my own men, I have turned to these as my only friends, and felt how much inferior to them was man when actuated only by selfish views.*

> *"We must not mistake the nature of the case: it is not because we train him to our use, and have made choice of him in preference to other animals, but because this particular species feels a natural desire to be useful to man, and, from spontaneous impulse, attaches itself to him. . . everywhere it is the dog only that takes delight in associating with us in sharing our abode; he is even jealous that our attention should be bestowed on him alone; it is he who knows us personally, watches for us, and warns us of danger.*

> *"It is impossible for the naturalist, when taking a survey of the whole animal creation, not to feel a conviction that this friendship between two creatures so different from each other must be the result of the laws of nature; nor can the humane and feeling mind avoid the belief that kindness to those animals from which he derives continued and essential assistance, is part of his moral duty."*

Then Goodrich went on, in his own words, to say:

> *"It may be truly said that the dog is the only animal capable of disinterested affection. The horse neighs that he may be fed; he enjoys the chase and*

feels emulation, and thus shares in some of our pleasures; but the dog desires to follow us, and be useful to us as a friend. He sacrifices his appetite and his liberty for our benefit. Queen Mary's lap-dog followed her to the scaffold, caressed the body when her head was cut off, and when forcibly withdrawn, pined away and died.

"The dog is as true in his affections in the midst of poverty as in abundance. He dines as cheerfully and thankfully on a bone with his pauper master, as on the ruddy roast beef of the lord of the manor. The instance of a cur that followed the body of his master, a poor tailor, to the churchyard of St. Olave, in London, and, refusing to be comforted, after a few weeks wasted away and perished, is familiar to all readers. There are innumerable instances of this sort. One of them, that of a young man who lost his life by falling from one of the precipices of the Helvellyn Mountains, and who for three months was guarded by his faithful dog—wasted at last to a skeleton—was even put into immortal verse by Scott".

INDEX

Page numbers printed in **bold** face refer to photographs